Aerialist

Mary Buchinger

ISBN 13: 978-0-692-34192-6
ISBN 10: 0692341926

Cover artwork: *Limelight* by Steve Barylick
Diptych, Oil stick on board, 12"x24" | 2014

Cover design: Brian Mihok
Author Photo: Tony Majahad

GOLD Wake Press
Boston, Mass.

Aerialist

This book is dedicated to all who meet together in cafes, libraries, living rooms, to read their work to one another, mulling over form and meaning.

Contents

I.

Was there no safety? No learning by heart of the ways of the world? No guide, no shelter, but all was miracle, and leaping from the pinnacle of a tower into the air?

Virginia Woolf, *To the Lighthouse*

How Precise, Joy and Melancholy

Marcel Proust, *Swann's Way*

In a sky of banded color—
pink and black as if ruled

a bird flies all pink pink air
draws near the terrible line

touches, enters
and *is lost*

The old red coop

was white inside
when I was young, the narrow
door swinging shut behind me
in a slam that rippled through
the round, nervy huddles.
The straw, hollow and rancid,
grew sharp in summer heat,
and I'd dare myself to breathe
with the hens, the hurried huff
of panted breath. One bloodied
pullet would bear it all. Feathers
rooted between my fingers,
none of us could fly.

Forgetting

Plato says we are born
    remembering,
and it is hard.

He knew the art
of *sgraffito*—scraping away
—and the beauty
    that lies beneath.

    ∎

My cousin's barn once held
farrowing sows on fresh straw.
We'd run inside to count
each new litter, guard the runts.
Now that barn floor is bare, grated,
slop runs into cisterns.
No sows, no runts, just lean pink hogs
    bought at forty,
        sold at two-twenty.

The thirty pieces of silver
descend again and again.

Judas, when he remembered,
turned to the trees.

▪

We get to ease Poe's Raven
out of the black squall Manet etched;
the stark scratch of claws
as if into skin.

Even more satisfying,
the chair that's barely there
in his sketch of *my soul*
from out that shadow
that lies floating on the floor
shall be lifted—nevermore!

Splendor—lilacs,
catalpas, strawberries—
summoned and spent,
the troubling of ink.

Yes, Plato, I remember,
help thou my unremembering

The Rape or Rapture of Europa

The gods always in disguise, nothing is as it seems.
Winged cupids tumble in the sky, dark scaly carp
nip fetlocks of the white bull. My own calf,
a ginger-and-cream Guernsey, chased me across
a velvet lawn in summer dusk. We didn't know then
the slant of light was meant for both of us.

I stroked the leathery nubs rising from his temples,
fingered the curling curls circling each. This,
his foreign warmth, my bliss when I was twelve.
Night after night, I spread hay in his manger,
shoveled oats, filled his water; the grooming,
the tantalizing give and take of needs to meet,
what this teaches a heart. (O blue-fanged carp, come
slip us up, flip the dangerous deep over our heads.)

Zeus came to Europa as a supple white beast,
offered his breast, its soft animal heat. Is this a brute
who loves? Dear child hands, run across the drum
of his ribs, convince me beneath revolving skies,
this creature is a god, this god will not leave.
Even so, I raised him for my father to kill
and I too ate his fat-marbled steaks.

and today Proust paints distance

glass jars—
            the village children

lower them
            into the Vivonne
for minnows

crystal containers of *flowing crystal*
            insoluble glass   *water impalpable*

      the fish flashing,
        caught and carried for bait

    come, time, come
bite,
                  that child-once-was
            that splash in a jar

Pietá

In the earliest paintings, the Madonna,
stiff in her perfection, the Baby, wooden,
neither of them soft, yielding; they are pink
or sallow, simple in contour. Clutched
in the infant's fist, a goldfinch that will peck
at agony's thorns, or an apple—the fruit
that brought Him here. As if unaware
of each other, They arrest and hold
your eye.
        That Mother, mysterious, iconic,
will be hauled down to earth, achieve perspective,
tenderness, and shadow as She enters realism, then
will disappear for some twenty years of His life.
As for Jesus, he will grow too large for her lap,
discover honey, wine, perfume; he will fish,
heal, preach, and finally be torn, pierced,
stinking of vinegar and blood, before
She will get to cradle Him again, both,
by then, gone supple with suffering.

Childhood, that nest

of gathered, broken sticks,
bark half-peeled, magic wands, lightning rods

winding, weaving like histories, down,
down to a sinking place, a holding,
hugging vortex filled
to swelling.

Nights I'd wake, restless, gaze into vastness beyond
the slight and airy edges of this messy assembly

so close to heaven and all its wishing stars,
a fall, so far.

Beauties

        exact pain from their familiars—
this, the world's logic, our contract with the sun:
welcome warmth, then scrape away the cancers

But, where is the place you go in those many seconds
of not knowing what's fluttering in nighttime's
streetlight—   leaf   moth   grandmotherly spirit

The dog says, *It's the memory I remember.*
Each time I check that spot where I once found food,
I rememorize.

II.

[Sambikin] immediately realized how much a human being is still a feebly constructed, homespun being—no more than a vague embryo and blueprint of something more authentic—and how much work must be done to unfurl from this embryo the flying, higher image buried in our dream.

Andrey Platonov, *Happy Moscow*

Apple

a little girl stands
beside an arching tree

looks up   points
that one   please Grandma

innocence   the red core
of improvisation

both actors here swing
vigorous on the hinge

of yearning   a mother
would never   too practical

busy   but   a grandmother
knows vulnerability   again

falls for   *that one   please*
desire   so   exact

fitting within a single skin
and thus   a chair gets pulled

from the patio   its four thin legs
meant for stone   not this

this soft   apple-pocked earth
steaming wasps

The first foundation

I knew intimately
held up my father's tall grey barn,
its rafters raised by German settlers
a hundred years before I was born.

I'd enter its dark on my stomach,
feeling for glass in the dirt—old beer bottles
the hired men had tossed between rough-hewn
timbers, thick as two of me.

Once within, I'd worm my arms down to my sides
and turn onto my back to face the knotted,
slatted floor above me, study a portion
of a worn tire of the John Deere.

Bandy roosters tip-tapped their way
across the floor looking for stray grain,
slipping a yellow claw now and then
down the narrow slits between planks.

And I'd stay in that dark place,
lying still, listening to creaks,
    the rasp of wood against wood,
        constant cooing of pigeons,

            low swoosh of darting swallow wings—
        the weight of the whole barn above me.
My knee hard up against a foundation rock,
I'd imagine I was that rock,

        cold, smooth, old as the earth,
with all that weight above pinning me down,
    and make myself stay there, stay, stay—
        until I could barely breathe.

The Heaven on Earth Campaign

A willowy girl at my gym has SCIENCE, in black
childish script, tattooed between her hip bones.
Another member of the club is becoming female—
male-chested and still shaving her beard,
her long pale hair leads the way like a vision.

Einstein said we're caught in a net linked across space,
the mass of all objects, from fleas to black holes, falls
inward, toward ever greater mass, warping everything,
making it impossible to define things separately—
"spooky" entanglement. *We are all responsible for all.*

Ospreys built a nest atop a construction crane in May,
halting work on the Anacostia, like the blackbird that
made a nest in young St. Kevin of Glendalough's hand
as he prayed, arms outstretched. She fed him nuts
and berries through Lent, till the hatchlings flew away.

"Redeem/The unread vision in the higher dream"

T.S. Eliot, *Ash Wednesday*

The pigeon lands on the sidewalk beside the raw graffiti'd wall, wings spread—each feather burning with sun—and I could swear I've seen that bird before. Then it comes to me: it's the Holy Ghost incarnate, the gold-tipped dove on church bulletins, flying low over the water, hovering over the head of Jesus in illustrated Bibles. The halo-making descent wipes clean the grey bird like he's learned something from Garbo and Leni Riefenstahl about the power of the right angle and light to suggest a godlike lurking. But the bird shifts and the Ghost is gone. Pink eyes and purple feet, blotchy bent feathers; and it's true, I know that bird too. What I mean to say is this: We all want, of course, that finest shot of ourselves, but what we need is someone with the eyes to look for it, to show us what it is. Someone who can position the grey pigeon in us just right, golden-up the edges— reminiscent of the holy—be blinded by our particular disturbance of the light.

The Latest Rapture

It's May and the end of this world is scheduled
for today. A young couple on the radio tells listeners
they're ready—sold everything, moved to Florida
with just enough to last them and their toddling
daughter until this Rapture, another baby due in June.
A transit worker who'd sunk his life-savings into
Judgment Day billboards waits it out in Times Square.

Someone on my street arranged a pair of old oxfords,
jeans and a shirt, all empty, neatly stretched out along
the cobblestones. Apocalypse easy as slipping out
of one's clothes. Weightless, untethered. Dostoyevsky,
too, was braced for the end, gambled for a jolt out
of the ordinary, craved a clean, uncomplicated slate—
Brothers Karamazov, the harvest of his disappointment.

Can endings live up to beginnings? This morning,
a plant swap at the community garden; I'll bring
pansies, hope for wild ginger. Later, Open Studios—

the artists baking cookies, assembling cheese plates
in anticipation. Stairwells cleared, everything matted
that's getting a mat, street corners marked by floating
balloons tied down with ribbons, the cheery bobbling
tells us where to turn.

"The Subject is a Long One"

Oscar Wilde, *in a letter about art*

What's that out-of-tune bee hive I hear, asks a giant man
spilling out of his white shirt and black suspenders.
Way down at the other end of the bus-station bench,
the skinny guy warming up his hurdy-gurdy leans over,
Out of tune what? And watching, you can't but know

this thing is his life that he's got strapped around
his shoulders, held dear, this wheel fiddle in rich red
and gold wood, lute-rose sound holes beside
the buzzing board and drone strings, a thing worn
and beloved, hazarded out to introduce

to the anonymous world. When the #73 pulls in,
the hurdy-gurdy's whine warbles my feet, and
everyone's, up the steps of the kneeling bus
to Watertown. Oscar Wilde (Oscar Fingal O'Flahertie
Wills Wilde) declared art useless because it only

creates a mood, useless as flower, as a touch (tender
kiss, breathy sigh), as a glass of chilled Chardonnay.
And moods, they do flounder, no sooner put your
finger on them and they disperse, disappearing
lightning bugs, darkly vacant as they once were bright.

On the bus, an old man jokes with a long blond
girl beside him. She replies, not a hint of a taunt,
Like to start all over again, ey? But no, the fiddle's
wheel only whiles the time, it is not useful,
just searching, sweet.

To the woman wrapped in a filmy scarlet scarf
sitting alone in the seat behind the driver,
I'm torn between, *Try not to cry among strangers,*
and, *There, there. The hurdy has the gurdy.*
They say everything unfolds like a flower.

On Your Birthday

Last summer's aster stands akimbo beneath a meeting
of roofs, sheathed in ice, its silver death at angles
to itself, caught unaware. The glassy arabesque stems
and bent petioles draw a cold sun and dazzle.

Its happenstance beauty knifes me. Friend, you are not
here. I walk slick narrows between hard snow banks;
a smooth sycamore limb in my reach—steady myself
or swing? I am every age I've ever been, recapitulating

again, again. Memory peeled back, your thumb
nudging as if to separate those capsuled moments
secreted away, tucked and ordered like hours in a day.
Why did you die so early, where are you?

We'd always found a place within a place, that
was our flair; how we labored to astonish, hoisting
rickety chairs up on cabinets, curled hair grazing
the ceiling as we girled our way toward womanhood.

That exquisite aster cannot shrug its ice alone.
I'm torn knowing you'd love the noise, the spectacle
of its splintering, but I say, leave it. The February sun
is growing teeth, let the weed come undone, bead

by bead, just as its translucent robe was woven.
See, we never did agree. Seeds scattered around
the stalk, their faces in dirt, poised to pulse.
I'll pretend to leave something of you

at your distant daughters' feet. I'm nothing
to them but a reminder of a life before theirs,
before death, nothing more than this flower
cloaked in aging winter's lace.

Bread Crumbs

Hansel and Gretel believed the bread crumbs were a mistake
because they didn't help them find their way back home.

Swedish fish and gummy bears, planted or slipping
untended through sleepy fingers to the ground, call
to the unfortunate children who follow, forbidden
to fingerhook the fruit animals dotting the sidewalk.
I imagine birds puzzled by the chewy crumbs—

■   ■   ■

We call it serendipity when it turns out well,
tragic when it doesn't.

Balancing zwieback and brie on my wrist—
Radcliffe poetry reception, elegant carpeted room,
white walls heavy with portraits. Everyone else
appears comfortable. A woman wanders over,
introduces herself, tells me her sisters and mother
graduated from here. I ask, How about you?
—Wellesley drop-out. A grandmother now,
she'll always be the one who dropped out,
especially here.

■   ■   ■

Tracing the dropping to the picking up is largely speculative.

I bought a ring at the consignment shop
mostly because I was told its former owner
was Middle Eastern and my country was
at war with Iraq.

Two days later a stone fell out,
leaving a tiny hole in the wall of the ring.

I bought earrings there too—also for their story.
The design, the shopkeeper explained, began
as a lover's gift; amulets and beads paired to win
a woman's love. Old metal and stone carrying old
blessings and protections, joined with new silver.
And then people, like me, who didn't even know him
were charmed and wanted to wear his creations.

But, I want to know—did it work?
Does she love him? Does he still love her?

．　　　　．　　　　．

We begin in one place, trying to do one thing.

Hansel and Gretel, you tried to ensure
your safe passage home, you used what you had,
the bread crumbs were just too tempting for others.
Still, didn't the songs of the grateful birds lessen
the hell of the witch's candied kingdom?

God scattered people to the winds—seeds
and ashes alike. Even God doesn't always play God.

Sometimes, I find myself thinking a stray comment
is foreshadowing. For instance, my seven-year-old son
asks, What would happen if a skier tried to go down
a perpendicular slope? He doesn't use the word
'perpendicular' but illustrates the straight up and down
with his hand—fingers forming an L with the top
of the table. I shudder. His father, whom I love,
is skiing, alone, today, and as I reassure him,

Daddy is careful and skilled (is that even what he's talking about?)

I remind myself that life is not art.

Except—it's true—we can look back as through photos of our younger selves and see, more or less, how we got here, where we are today.

We wander through the cemetery

birds string along their watchers
  glide between trees
    gaze back into binoculars

My great-aunt Lois died at ninety
  my friend says

star magnolias flutter helplessly
  edges beginning to pucker and rust
not quietly at home, as one would expect

new maroon minnows
  stipple the pond surface
    but in the backseat of a stranger's car

red-winged blackbirds fret
  cry, dive at ducks and frogs
because her car had caught fire

in the shadowy dell
  a dogwood pauses
on a Sunday country outing

limbs poised for blossom
with her beau, Old Sid

at its heart, a sunken hole
pursed-lipped vernal pool
and they'd had to walk almost a mile

yellowy insects scuttle
through its mossy beard
You met her at my wedding, she tells me

the mildewed earth
clambers up
from winter's basement

a strum of fiddleheads
A good woman.

every life

begins
with a map of this day:

dark
   growing into light
      drawn back
      again to
dark

the arc
   all but
brushes
   up against
      the apocalyptic

black shine
   mirror
      of a seed
reveals the grain
   of sun
      rains

green
   to gold
    back
to rich rot
black

map of stone
   from wet hot
lava
   ends too
     soft broken
           dust
     ready to be
wet
  again

the map
  grows full

    grows
  simple

Airborne

One windy day in March, two months before
her eighty-ninth birthday, my grandmother,
standing at her south window, caught sight
of her trash can lid skipping across the yard.
Naturally, she pulled on her coat and headed out.

She'd fought disorder all her life in that flat square
mile where she'd been born and lived out her years.
Yet, profound intimacy with the land and its
eccentricities hadn't prepared her for the experience
of being suddenly airborne, lifted up, off the ground.

The howling wind, didn't know, of course, what
it was doing, who it was handling. This is what prayers
are for, to talk some sense into these acts of God.
Thankfully, she came out of it well enough. Bruised,
her ancient porcelain bones intact, she returned

to her velveteen recliner by the window, beside
petite pots of African violets, to record the event
in her diary. No mention of feeling lighter or winged,
no question of her substantiality. The scamp lid rolled
across a few acres of winter wheat, landed in a ditch.

As odd incidents do, it gave her something
to talk about and for her granddaughter,
who'd long left that square mile, to ponder
years after it had happened, years after her
grandmother had flown completely away.

III.

Time is a river that sweeps me along, but I am the river; it is a tiger that mangles me, but I am the tiger; it is a fire that consumes me, but I am the fire. The world, unfortunately, is real; I, unfortunately, am Borges.

Jorge Luis Borges, *A New Refutation of Time*

Morning, February

In this conspiracy of white—
white sky, white earth

—the trees suggest
the tangle above
is no different
from the tangle below

that it is one single act
of grope and delve,
the excavation of air
and stubborn ground.

Magnificat

PixCell-Elk#2
sculpture by Kohei Nawa

In a gallery in   Australia   I
found   a   honey-yellow elk covered in
thousands of glass   bubbles.   The
bubbled beads cupped patches of fur
circles of ear   hoof   snout
roughed-up horn.
          The elk   inside   dead but
shining.
                              Inhaling light
the glass   bent   the fluorescence to
magnify like Mary for Elizabeth the
gorgeousness at the very surface of the
blank and terrible.

Unveiling

A man on the subway sketches a woman
across the aisle who happens to sit beneath a
map of the Red Line. She's donned the veil of
morning commuters, indrawn and elsewhere,
even as her face—cheekbones and sunken
eyes—emerges in graphite from his smooth
paper. His wrist and forearm move—back,
forward, around—with quick, controlled
strokes, as the train stops and starts again,
again, Harvard, Central, Kendall, filling with
passengers carrying briefcases and backpacks,
newspapers open like wings, still he manages
a sightline, draws the thin bow of her lips—if
she could see this, surely she'd recognize
herself—ringlets of dark hair, pierced lobe of
her right ear. As the train lifts to cross the
river, it's almost quiet—the noise springs
clear, the light so much larger out here.

Aerialist in the Subway Car

She rises from her seat beside me,
loosens the stanzas of her spine,
and composes faith from the grey
everyday hand-straps above our heads,
meant for the standing-only.

Arms summoning a choir of muscle,
she draws herself up into a hymn I've always
dreamt of singing, and dangles upside-down
like a whole note, inches from the lit ceiling
that has never before looked so habitable.

Her torso sways, measures time
as the rest of us forget breath, then
this clef of a woman unfurls and returns
to sit like one who would not consider calling
into question the dogma of the commute.

Having just taught us all to pray,
she faces straight ahead, closes her eyes,
and the air fills with a hum of *this, too,
is possible*, and oh, may we all be held
upright, firm in devotion to our art.

Reading Signs

Waiting for a diagnosis, no walk is innocent
or aimless. I seek tessellations everywhere—between
small dull stones in noncommittal dirt, in leaves done
being green, ready to detach.

Sometimes though, I forget, and begin
to wonder how cobalt blue tiles might look
above my kitchen sink. How small a question.

Everyone lives here sometime. Still, we fix
our bowls of oatmeal, help the kids with homework,
feed the dog, clean the tub. It's not as if we have
certainty ever about anything, yet, we convince
ourselves to rise from our beds each morning.

■

A Japanese student lands at Boston Logan Airport,
midday on 9/11, shows up downtown, at my door.
I'd just escorted four Saudi women from my class

to the train, their silky head-scarves stashed
in backpacks. The young man from Tokyo
speaks no English, needs help finding a place
to stay. Together we walk stunned streets
of Boston, his giant neon-yellow suitcase
bouncing on cobblestones as we pass
the flashing fire engines and ambulances
flanking Beacon Hill.

Planes hit New York and Washington D. C., I tell him,
people have been killed, the U.S. is under attack.
He nods with a smile, bows, opens his palms
to the heavens, and shrugs.

When I get home that afternoon, our Indian neighbor
has taped, on every window of her apartment,
tricolored printouts of the United States flag.

∎

It's all incidental here, except maybe the way
an oak or maple spreads, each branch reaching out
just a bit for an extra slice of sun. Individual limbs
forging ahead, leaf by leaf, stomata opening to harvest
the light, vessels of xylem ferrying water and minerals,
phloem filling with sap to feed the rings,
pocketed industry pulsing inside,

but when we stand back, what do we see?
Symmetry, balance, a geometric sum—as if tuned
to a spectrum beyond. And look, two trees,
the skinny-leaved ash heaving up the sidewalk
and the dense blue spruce in my inconsequential yard,
how they work it out—forging a whole,
even as they compete for sky.

Hospital Wallpaper Pastoral

You find yourself on a strange table,
lying on your stomach for long minutes,
head turned, with nothing
but flowered wallpaper to examine.
One arm up, elbow crooked,
but not beneath your head
(your hand would fall asleep)
and the other arm down along your side,
parts of you hanging exposed,
accessible to others.

The paper pattern is satisfyingly complicated,
allowing you to move
from flower to flower, depending.
Just as you expand into the yawning
pale yellow hibiscus
comes the command (always a surprise):
Hold Your Breath
and immediately, you draw yourself up
into those tiny blood-red buds
in the corner.

Now You Can Breathe　and there you are,
the spray of opened crimson flowerets.
Once again, you dare to make your way past
the pendulous folded bud,
and on into the showy golden blossom.

So it goes, as they tug and handle you from below
You Will Feel A Pinch—;
no warning of the cool alcohol,
the marker sliding across your skin,
the probing, the sudden micro-bursts of lidocaine.

Only when they count down
Three-Two-One-Zero!
for the noisy pop of the machine
does a warm arm drape itself across
your shoulders—restraint or comfort,
it doesn't matter, it's warm. Your eyes trail along
the stems that wind themselves into ivy leaves
and branches, and you dip, with each urgent,
odd activity, into a waiting flower.

What then would be malignancy here—everything
means something, you've established that much—
the neutral, blank background on which this scene
in contrast plays, or the very network of green
on which all manner of flowering depends?

A friend asks how I am

Just as I open my mouth to answer,
Proust interrupts—*what lay hidden*
behind the steeples of Martinville must
be something analogous to a pretty phrase

and I leave it at that, the day ending
and beginning at the horizon,
a horizon hidden behind streets
and steeples, the how I am,

something analogous out beyond,
worthy of this effort,
of the imagination it takes
to walk the day away from me.

Not that it was, but

The familiar desire
not to have been disappointed
made me think it beautiful—

writes Proust. Desire girds
me too, a waving shield of ivy
against an old brick wall.

Livid impatiens, moss roses,
flashbulb-bright snapdragons
temper their dirt as they swing

in plain brown plastic pots.
The sun climbs morning,
birds pull taffy from cerulean air,

the tree of heaven no one planted
leans its terrible long lean—
menace to neighboring yards,

yet how pretty the tree's spangle
of tiny buds, curving limbs
open to an opalescent dove.

Catching an Early Flight

It's four in the morning and the cabbie
corners my eye in the mirror before he starts
the story in his cigarette-raked voice, and
I can see her just how he saw her, the woman
both silky and sad in the back of his cab
those years ago, how many, he doesn't say.
How his day became hers, as they left the city
and headed north to New Hampshire.

Her directions so tentative he wondered
if he could trust her to bring them to some place
definite. How the yellow cottage waited
at the end of a dirt road, hunched up beneath
its dripping forest. Rainy and cold, the day
half gone, the meter long switched off,
she asked him in. Even as he built her a fire
and she opened the wine, it was all a question.

Sometimes still he wonders if it was a dream,
and it's as if he's reading my mind, my own dream
of those roads that unravel past empty fields,
the strangeness of longing or whatever brought her

to his cab that day. The story, finished, sits between us
in the dark quiet, we're the only two people awake
in the world, our lit car nosing toward the elegant
bridge, into the deeper city, its coil of concrete streets.

Sitting on a Bench in St. Pete

I want to see art.

For instance, that man with the tanned
potbelly, tattoo rippling on his bicep, long grey hair
sweeping his shoulder as he walks along the pier
holding a casting net. With a sinker from its weighted
fringe held between his lips, he twirls, balletic
on his bare feet atop the narrow wall. The net opens
like a lung, gulps water, then is pulled up, dripping.
Such ease and grace, authority in his working figure.

An old guy and his younger, smoking
companion come along the path, *Honey, we didn't walk
this far.* (Beat.) *Lost car!* she announces, as if to recruit
support. Her too-blonde hair glows like a beacon.
They wander up and down Beach Front Drive.

A leashed chihuahua clips by, oblivious
as his mini-skirted Olive Oyl owner. Sailboats blush
in the early April sunset. *What does it look like,* Beacon
Blonde asks. This is their third pass. *It's almost
a Mercedes,* he says. She takes his keys, waves them

like a wand, presses panic with her thumb. For a long
time, they don't pass by again.

They remind me of the rare lithograph
I saw in an antique store earlier today, Napoleon with
his son. Napoleon, in full uniform, sits on a draped
sofa in a study filled with books, paintings, statues;
he is tense, a map in his hand, as if this too, his
battlefield, commander-in-chief of the domestic scene.
His son flows beside him, a pale eel with his golden
head on the stiff white pillow of the military thigh.
Nothing paternal there.

The couple is back again, he's saying,
Your memory's better than mine. She replies, *I had too,
too many mojitos.* Both Napoleon and this couple
carry on, at odds with their circumstances.

Meanwhile, the fisherman enters
the water, the calm shallows darken his jeans,
his whirled net spreads, transparent as a jellyfish,
rounding the water, stretched out and open
to capture the necessary bait.

Earrings I Never Wear

In a small Bolivian town
on a narrow cobblestone path,
a woman in a black bowler hat
and white embroidered blouse
sits at a tiny tin table in front
of her sky-blue house selling
shiny things that would catch
a magpie's eye. I finger the glitter,

but it's the earrings she's wearing
I want—articulated fish, worn
brass, warped, greenish, hinged
with rings, a head, tail, fins.
Do you have any like those
for sale, I ask. She shakes
her head as she pulls them
from her lobes. *My husband*
made these, they take the extra
air out of your head, make it
possible to breathe. Best earrings
for a headache. She says this
as she thrusts them into my palm
and my head begins to throb.

No, I say, they're yours,
your husband made them,
they heal you, keep them,
please, I only wondered
if there were any others—
These, please. Buy these.
Already in my hand,
they curl up and die.

The Midway at the County Fair

All colors of balloons line up
for the popping. A dart thrust between your fingers—
was it always this dull?—bouncing off a ball of air,
and, oh! the plastic yellow ducks, Pick one, just one
from the shallow circling stream, don't wish too hard
for a special prize, just dream of a lucky number,
dream.
                                    Bright buckets
swing to and fro on a giant wheel, couples sway,
suspended between up and down. You too, one time
with a boy who wanted your silver abalone ring.
You traded for a cheap crucifix
that turned your neck green,
                          and the Alpine rollercoaster,
its tin circle of twelve-foot mountains, royal blue and
gold, topped with white snow paint, cars jerking along
a rackety track. Once you stood at its gate,
hand-in-hand with your mother, judging the ride
against your ages,
                          faithful Tilt-a-Whirl
you'd turn to for a taste of chaos,
the hard, curved seat and the metal bar

that you held, that held you, its illusion
of control, cheery shells,
twirling red hollows.

The midway is where
you see lemonade squeezed direct from the press,
syruped and iced, apples candied and hot dogs
dressed up as if that's not what you wanted at all,
disguise for the bit you desire the most, isn't that
how it really is?

And you fall out of line
for a smell that takes you back, even if you didn't
love it before, it means too much to you now,
poignant and laden. Striped straws, pink gum
litter the dirt.

It's shrunken, this acre of carnies, bare wires
and bulbs, white sheds, weathered, peeling. Sun
explodes the growing knotholes. The front of each
little building, hinged in the middle: one door up
and one door down become the window and the tray
for your popgun. Stuffed animals dangle, fuzzed
and worn, dust on the tail.

Call, Me, Ishmael

Call: What is to name; to disambiguate; to wrestle some small control over what is otherwise formless; what is to beckon, as in a dog or a God, verbal equivalent (in some cultures) of the index finger pointing and hooking inward; what is a kind of nomination; acknowledgement of existence, whose very existence depends upon such acknowledgement.

Me: What is deictic, shifting; what is myself; what is "everyone," assuming atomic relation (W. Whitman); what is "absolutely   not   You" (A. Notley); what is time, tiger, fire (J. L. Borges); what is he who goes to sea when feeling at sea (H. Melville); what is the speaker, persona, voice, author (e.g., M. Buchinger).

Ishmael: What is a name that names, equal parts arbitrary and motivated; what is Biblical: wayward son of Abraham, both chosen and rejected, victim of Divine caprice (what is another way of understanding our lives); what is a nominal predicate which, while proper, shares with every word in every language, the possibility of being actual, provisional, and/or false.

IV.

"It is time for the century of the rat to end and the century of the swallow to begin," the more determined said. *In fact, already beneath the grim and petty rattish dominion, you could sense, among the less obvious people a pondering, the preparation of a swallowlike flight, heading for the transparent air with a deft flick of the tail, then tracing with their wings' blade the curve of an opening horizon.*

Italo Calvino, *Invisible Cities*

The Decision I Wake To This Morning

The sky is torn by dark birds,
a ragged azure flag through which they circle,
balled fists, black umbrella wings.

Men below follow the tight formation
with lifted rifles, metal tips spiraling
as if held by strings from the beaks above.

Shots.

One bird stutters in flight, stalls,
I watch it fold and drop,
tilt into earth.

I run away—*It's going to fall on me!*
but the men yell, *Catch it!*
so I turn back to where it lies on dirt.

I kneel down, hold its wings close
to the pumping body,
stroke the speckled brown sheen,

how small the wounded.
How to assess suffering
in something so other.

Should I, must I, take in hand
this delicate neck,
downy with feather?

Natural History

I balance in sandals on flagstone
at a backyard party far from home, where only
the hosts know me. Colorado's Flat Irons
and Red Rocks press against a darkening sky,
far-off mountains scallop the purple and gold wads
of clouds.
      Nearby, twin boys carry bugs in cups—praying
mantises praying their separate ways along grassy,
plastic interiors. Their mother, pleased, bends low
in a linen sundress beside her awkward, matching
boys, inspects what they hold.
      One mantis is green,
the other brown—male and female, guess the twins.
Or, their mother offers, maybe one's young, the other,
old. *Let's look it up!* Her phone in hand,
they won't have to wonder.
      She tells me she analyzes
sentiment, writes computer programs to find out how
people feel about things. I write about how
this feels—the balancing, accounting
for difference.

This morning, in the cool
of the University's Museum, I counted forty
stuffed chipmunks lined up, head to tail, for a story
of variation in their tiny pelts, the slips of their backs
arranged small to large to small, their stripes,
individual, stationary.
                    But out here, the sky moves,
always lightning at day's end, a summer heaven
full of distance, of crackling, toothed light
chasing after dark.

That Old Story

A flurry of spiderlings
bursts out of their silken capsule

one nearly transparent speck-with-legs
        separates from the white feverish pack

alights on the page of an open book

        circles as if to make out the meaning
of the marks

        none of this in her vocabulary
            she moves on

    taking her frenzy
        to the sheer grey
            of the desk lamp

    then scrambles up again
        on her new web
            this simple *y* she's made

she scurries down

      up

   down

  up this shining filament

of hers

as if to make sure
   it really happened—

         this emerging

The Way Things Fall

My young sons toss maple helicopter seeds
off the second-story deck, mesmerized
by the way they pedal the air as they fall,
one-finned fish cutting spirals in a watery sky.

Before each is dropped, it's named:
> *Old Man Plum Picker.*
> *She-Boom-She-Ba.*

I study the fan of veins rising from one barely green
seed-heart, how it spreads thin and thinner, fringing
fingers webbed with a papery membrane to wing away
the weight of the circumscribed seed, and I feel

the unfurling of my children,
of this moment beneath a lean sun.
I name as much as I can before letting it go,
the play of light—*such pretty shapes!*—falling.

Mussel Girl

I barely get my chair set up on the beach when a
chubby little girl adopts me as if she hadn't
noticed my very own boisterous boys racing into
the water seconds before. She ignores my open
book and chats away, no parents, no siblings in
sight, as if she'd exhausted everybody, and then
she's bringing me mussels, sweet-water mussels,
by the handful, "See? They're having a party!"
Dozens of mussels—"This one's a baby!"—
shrivel beside me in the sun-burnt sand.

Dead Seal at State Beach

Damp ruffled patch of sand, long white bones
rib-rows

and one bleached cupping blade
all the rest, dark

maggots, cool and moving as the iris of an eye
seething their own sea

an unseen hand undulates, lifting
the mantle of them

they teem
incidental syncopation

tiniest movement, concert
of mouths

like the peppery waves
that chiseled rock into this swallowing sand.

I kneel beside
the ticking orbit, spindle of ends.

In a Spring of War and Rumors

I cut my son's hair   Good Friday early April
just warm enough
to take the scissors and stool outside

I dip my comb into a glass of tepid water
run it through all   the   colors of gold
the sun speaking   differently to   each   strand

His hair   glistens   wet and darker
lines up   attentive to the spines
of the black rat-tail comb

And then   the violence I do—
sliced half-curls lie in clumps
on my red wool slippers

Thin spokes of cut hair catch light
drift among leafless trees   mark the slightness
of the breeze   This—   these—   can never

be re-gathered   perhaps a few strands
will find their way into nests   the rest   fodder
for the open mouth of earth

Icarus falls every day

shards of gold slice sky
as the dome lifts
from an ivory mosque

planes fly coffins home
stars in a fabric night
fold into triangles

we sort the mail
pet the cat, crush garlic
plunge pasta into the boil

feathers and melted wax
a boy falling out of the sky
as we sit down to supper

Self-Portrait with Desk Lamp

Inside, Pärt's *Magnificat* and *Nunc Dimittis* battle
with the noise of a sewer sucker outside the blinded
den windows; radio nattering in the kitchen.
Today's expert on Talk of the Nation warns
bananas may become a thing of the past,
the seedless clones threatened by a fungus, so
the show's host cues up, "Yes! We Have No
Bananas" and invites stories from listeners
poised for nostalgia, like the missionary
who picked bananas from his own tree
in Africa. Shall I call in to tell about
my friend's husband coming home sick
each night from the banana fields, poisoned
by fungicide? 70,000 pounds of explosives
were dropped this morning in a rural area of Iraq;
I grew up in a rural area. Nine American deaths
reported. Ten of my muscle groups were worked
earlier today, each highlighted for me in a drawing
of a man's body on the weight machine, striated
muscles splayed out in purple, across his shoulders
and thighs—*latissimas dorsi, gluteus medias*. Before
leaving the gym, I offered salutations to the sun,

then headed out into rain, a thunderstorm misplaced
in a northern January, and now, here I am,
switching on the grey lamp beside me,
its springs taut, the cup of light tipped back
and down to cut the glare.

Raw Materiel

boys
girls
fresh
skin
friable
hair
iron
fences
iron shards
rip skin rip fences
more skin more iron
more shards
fences
iron
hair
friable
skin
fresh
girls
boys

An Abstract on Grief

A   certain   speed   of   wind   blowing
over   a   certain   distance   a   considerable   length
of   time
essentially   indeterminate   *creates   lasting   waves*
never going   any   where.

No   station   no schedule   an   Ocean
stirring   occasionally furious   falling   one   hardly
algebraic
into   the other   how   deep
not   reckoned
moving   only   not   moving.

Some   waves   undergo   a   phenomenon   called breaking
when   the base can   no   longer   support
if   the slope   if   the   steepness
if   the depth-

to- height   ratio is   too great
collapse.

Torn
or   is   it   toppled

87

falling   connection
pulls   inevitably
down   this linking   void

     linking of *seas:*
created   when the wind   has blown   for a while
time's hinge *at a given velocity.* Seas   last
much   longer   even   after
                  the wind sinks
and builds and building still until *swells: waves*
that have moved away
   from their area of origin

oblivious to local conditions u n d w e l l i n g —

in   other words
     in technical   terms
in the language available   *swells are*

seas rummaging   *lasting*
   lasting   *long*   knitted *beyond*

At the Reception

We stand at a small cocktail table,
our plates of tabbouleh and brie
nearly touching. He has every right
to tell his story, yet we want it
not to belong anywhere.

A scholar of African literature, he travels
outside his country to teach. One day
he returns, gets called in by the Chief,
they'd gone to school together, known
each other since they were boys. No,
he tells this man, I did not bring guns
from Denmark. No, no thousands
of soldiers. His accuser falls asleep.

Eventually he's led to another room,
left by himself for hours. When two men
come to ask for his belt and shoes,
he knows. The torture is in the morning.
Or the afternoon. It's in the night.
Sometimes many times. He doesn't know

his wife is writing letters, colleagues
all over the world are writing letters.

Amnesty persists, where are these guns,
where these soldiers? At the bottom
of his cell door, a hole large enough
for the rats. At this point, the third person
standing at our little table, silent until now,
clears her throat and asks, In your country,
do they speak English? He answers politely,
as if this question follows naturally.

But none of this belongs. It's been four years.
His wife's still there. In spring, the old
are born. The young experience death.
The lamb and the lion take turns.
This April morning sparkles, cold.
The magnolias froze. Taxes are due.
Last night, I dreamt my tongue was numb.

Spilling

sky scis-
    sor'd

    bird
  by bird
      then bird

a party of purple
           mums
        warning

  deciduous   death   again

the needle
      bed
    tawny
  tinder

   ■

even cut
    blue does not   wave

nor wander

but, look, one small
      winged being
    hosts   light

shepherds
    its given sun

shivering—

    against
        what?

    everyday
          wind
or
  be it

that
    diminishing
      cup?

White Space, Interrupted

Black vine charcoal trees stretch into the snow
of the page. This, a new page the artist borrowed
for the day to carry what it can. Bear in mind, none
of this was here before; it's wrong to want more.

These stark trees hold the delicate white easily
and keep it clean; each branch, a separate thought.
Fallen bits of coal track the snow into moth-light
deep inside the wooly shadow of low bushes.

A penciled-in pond stands ready to absorb
its blankness, and its undoing. In a ring around
the pond's rim, slips of cattails lean against
one another, remind us beauty is poor sustenance.

In the bottom corner, a small white bowl,
outlined by snow, grips stones in a clasp of ice.
The only touch of pastels—what can happen
when we forget what we'd planned—

coral and malachite stones from sand-blown
shores far-away, their accidental color
a language with little sense here, but assume
it has rules, that it too can be learned.

V.

And we—unlike circus acrobats,
conjurers, wizards, and hypnotists—
can fly unfledged,
we light dark tunnels with our eyes,
we wax eloquent in unknown tongues,
talking not with just anyone, but with the dead.

Wisława Szymborska, *Dreams*

New Year's Eve Afternoon

Avon Hill lifts its houses again and again, up
and over the shoulders of other old houses,
each household strange as mine walled within.
This salmon pink Victorian with its sturdy door,
stucco exterior beginning to crackle, lichen creeping
up the edges—let's walk by it again, Dover.
I tug her leash, redirect her fervent pursuits,

and the house unfolds like a revelation,
something here about the new year, or the old one,
in its turret, its bubbled glass, garden entry sinking
sideways, staked roses wrapped against winter,
grey granite cobblestones in the walkway bucking up
against each other, against original intentions, but
following laws, particles acting how they must,
patches visible as interruptions, efforts, a series of cuts
and stitches—what we inherit, what we work
ourselves into.

There are lives in that house
accumulating in its moldering darkness, and I will
never know them, will barely know my own.
Dover nudges my hand, proposes we move on.

Old Wasp Nest

conical, crisp, suspended from the beech tree—
abandoned? Early spring, sun's warmth, essential
and burgeoning; breeze, lined with coolness. Sturdily
attached, the nest extends and twirls the grey of the
small branches holding it; raggedy along the edges,
flaps coming undone, but still, for being what it is
—fibers from dead wood, plant stems mixed with
wasp saliva—how tenacious and substantial
to be here in April, no leaves on the trees
anymore or yet.   Old mother of aging
children. To extricate this nest from its
twining, and shake, however gently,
always, even long after it's sure
to be empty, the worry
of what might
wake.

.

When dreaming

      —I awake to spring and rain,
the locust in the window leans toward birds.
A sifting light collects what may remain.

I reach for me and then I reach again,
within the skin, an emptiness stirs.
When dreaming, I awake to spring and rain.

We see by closing eyes. What do we contain?
The child at every age, the rest, just words.
A shifting light contends with what remains.

The kitchen table wobbles, its wood scuffed, stained
yet holds a glass of water curving earthward.
When dreaming, I awake to spring and rain.

My breakfast crumbs, cat's purr—can these be chains?
I trace the links, as the here of me blurs.
A shimmery light conceals what may remain.

The sparrow opens wings and drops sustained; air,
her ground; my cage of seeds, her cupboard.
When dreaming, I awake to spring and rain.
A sifting light collects all that remains.

The South-Facing Room

Accept that you have to start
with the thin line of the hard lead,
its stray marks easier to coax away.

Sketch only space. Cleave contour.
Erase what you know. Look again.
Line meets line meets light, reveals

your draft—its pip, all angle and arc.
Now, move on to the soft graphite,
arbiter of dark, and forage for hollows.

Sweeps and hatches deepen a crevice,
draw you fearless into corners, arrange
for you objects levitating from shadow.

Finally, reach for color: fire, blue-heart petals,
bright spines of books, a lemongrass wall.
Elaborate that page until night falls.

Vernal Equinox

This is how it happens: a dinner of
leftovers and fresh-baked biscuits, then
the kids scamper upstairs, telling us to
wait at the table as a March storm draws
circles of snow outside, full-bodied
ghosts of winter coiling narrow white
sleeves up to bare maple limbs caught in
the wind, then our boys descend again
and turn out the lights on us, only the
snow glows sodium-orange through the
dining room windows, Stravinsky's
Infernal Dance of King Kashchei on
the stereo, our sons announce
themselves transformed into the River
Spirit and the Shadow of Death, strange
figures spiraling black-gowned legs and
arms, flinging dark selves into dark,
trading shadows swirl for swirl, while
we parents murmur be careful, watch
out, covering sharp corners of the table
with our hands, the boys giggle,

spinning on the wooden floor, the
bigger one lifts the younger into the air,
up toward the old chandelier of copper
bees, homemade pennon flapping
above a shaky pirouette of brothers,
the swift current of our twined rivers
sweeping them, oh cold ache, these wild
living gods of death, whirling, whirling,
too   fast   it   goes.

Like estuaries, we live on tides

How long ago he and I entered

this science
of channels, zones, torrents

The erosion of rock
creation of sand and gravel

We don't speak of accretion inside bends
nor of meanders

We take care not to lull or eddy
near the subterranean
those dank caves and caverns—

And yes, we've known
how it is
to be ephemeral

But coupled
    water learns this too:
        rivers braid
           at the beds of glaciers
        (that long, old cold)
        and flow uphill
           —uphill

Oh, we are years of water together
           swift
           against
        the narrowest banks

living the law of Brahm and Airy:
        the faster we go, my Love,
          the more we can carry

And lazing, too, ox-bowed, sinuous
    inviting picnics
        beside
           our violets and loosestrife,
            pale banks of meadow rue.

Island Dreamed

You breathe wet grey,
grey of water and sky, and it sucks you in,
monotone of being. Standing on a watery path

above the perpetual ocean's edge, you know
you must choose a destination, only one,
each equidistant from your heart:

you can head north, where the grey sky swirls
with wild bursts of silent fireworks, or south
to the world's only marble lighthouse. You imagine

the white stone column, a singular idea constructed
whole, while the lively, luminous riot beckons you
from the other shore. Beneath your feet, roots of trees

hold rainwater in their snarl. You spy, in the mud,
a small piece of paper, officious with numbers
and an oval portrait that makes you think of God.

Look, you say, *Money*, but foreign, outdated,
the one and many zeros, worthless everywhere; still,
this is something, and you slip it into your pocket.

On the river's edge

geese float like speckled seeds.
Later, they will sprout wings, leave
the naked frogs tumbling in the current.

The geese sip air and water alike, press against
the liquids, they too feel the ice
in the upper sky, suspended, crystallized.

They say, We live in two places at once,
Hwaann! Hwaann! You too. You too.

NOTES

Section quotes:

I. Virginia Woolf, *To the Lighthouse*, San Diego: Harcourt Brace Jovanovich.

II. Andrey Platonov, *Happy Moscow*, translated by Robert and Elizabeth Chandler, New York: New York Review Books.

III. Jorge Luis Borges, "A New Refutation of Time" in *Selected Non-Fictions*, edited by Eliot Weinberger; translated by Esther Allen, Suanne Jill Levine, and Eliot Weinberger. New York: Viking.

IV. Italo Calvino, *Invisible Cities*; New York: Harcourt Brace Jovanovich.

V. Wisława Szymborska, "Dreams," Translated from the Polish by Clare Cavanagh and Stanislaw Baranczak, *Poetry*, September 2010.

"How Precise, Joy and Melancholy," "and today Proust paints distance & memory," "a friend asks how I am," and

"Not that it was, but" are based on passages from *Swann's Way* by Marcel Proust; the C.K. Scott Moncrieff and Terence Kilmartin translation, revised by D. J. Enright.

"Forgetting" includes a quote from Edgar Allan Poe's poem, "The Raven," as well as a reference to illustrations by Édouard Manet for Stéphane Mallarmé's French translation of "The Raven" in 1875.

"The Rape or Rapture of Europa" references the painting, *Europa*, by Titian (Tiziano Vecellio), oil on canvas, Isabella Stewart Gardner Museum, Boston, Massachusetts.

The title of "The Heaven on Earth Campaign" comes from *The Brothers Karamzov* by Fyodor Dostoyevsky; it is also his character, Alyosha Karamazov, who declares, *We are all responsible for all*. The Anacostia Riverwalk Trail Project was put on hold for several weeks when a pair of ospreys built a nest on a construction crane in May, 2011. St. Kevin of Glendalough is said to have been seven years old when a blackbird built her nest in his hand as he was praying.

"Magnificat" describes the sculpture *PixCell-Elk#2,* by Kohei Nawa; taxidermied elk, glass, acrylic, crystal beads, Queensland Gallery of Art, Brisbane, Australia.

"Sitting on a Bench in St. Pete" refers to the painting, *Napoleon & Son,* by Karl August Steuben (1788-1856).

"Icarus falls every day" borrows the line "a boy falling out of the sky" from W. H. Auden's poem, "Musee des Beaux Arts," based on the painting, *The Fall of Icarus,* by Pieter Brueghel; oil-tempera, Museum of Fine Arts, Brussels, Belgium.

"Self Portrait with Desk Lamp" mentions music by Arvo Pärt's, an Estonian composer of classical and sacred music. "Talk of the Nation" was an American talk radio program, produced by National Public Radio. The song, "Yes! We Have No Bananas," composed by Frank Silver and Irving Cohn, is from the 1922 Broadway revue *Make It Snappy.*

"An Abstract on Grief" includes quotes from the entry for Wind Wave in Wikipedia.

ACKNOWLEDGEMENTS

Grateful acknowledgment is due to the editors of the following publications in which these poems, some in different versions, first appeared:

AGNI: "The Subject is a Long One"
AGNI Online: How Precise, Joy and Melancholy;
    and today Proust paints distance
and/or: Beauties
Booth: A Journal: The First Foundation
Caesura: Icarus falls every day
Dash: Unveiling
DIAGRAM: Call, Me, Ishmael; every life
Ekphrastia Gone Wild, Poems Inspired by Art: Magnificat
Existere (Canada): White Space, Interrupted
Fifth Wednesday Journal: New Year's Eve Afternoon
491 Magazine: Island Dreamed (as, On the Island
    Dreamed)
Ibbetson Street: The Midway at the County Fair
Nimrod International Journal of Prose and Poetry: Bread
    Crumbs
Orbis (England): On Your Birthday
OVS: Aerialist in the Subway Car
PANK: The Heaven on Earth Campaign

Salamander: Earrings I Never Wear

She Did It Anyway Anthology: That Old Story

Soundzine: We wander through the cemetery

The Cortland Review: Pietá; Dead Seal on State Beach

The Examined Life: Literary Journal of the University of Iowa Carver College of Medicine: Hospital Wallpaper Pastoral

The Massachusetts Review: "Redeem / The unread vision in the higher dream"

The William and Mary Review: The South-Facing Room

Two Thirds North (Sweden): At the Reception; Vernal Equinox

Upstairs at Duroc (France): An Abstract on Grief; Raw Materiel

Wilderness House Literary Review: Mussel Girl (as, "Girl at the Beach")

Words to Cure the Tameness (Ed. Sara Biggs Chaney; Special Issue, *Right Hand Pointing*): Apple; The old red coop

Award

Firman Houghton Award, New England Poetry Club: Airborne

For their patience, encouragement, insight, and careful attention, I'm profoundly indebted to Hilary Sallick and Linda Haviland Conte, Adnan Adam Onart and Bob Brooks, Susan Donnelly, David Semanki, Afaa Weaver, Victor Howes, Jane Attanucci and Marjorie Thomson, Philip Burnham and Ruth Smullin, Martha Collins, Chloe Martin, K.T. Landon, Edmund Jorgenson, Molly Bennett, and so grateful to David Tanner for saying, *Go ahead, write!* Special thanks to Kyle McCord and Nick Courtwright for their expertise and assistance, and to Jared Wahlgren for selecting this manuscript. Love and gratitude always for my guys—Steve, Liam, and Kai.

About the cover artist: Steve Barylick has a BFA in Painting from Massachusetts College of Art and a Certificate in Art History from the School of Fine Arts at Boston University. After a 30-year career as an art and creative director, he returned to painting in 2007. His paintings have been selected for juried exhibitions and exhibited in galleries in and around Boston, New York, Provincetown, Rochester, NY; Providence, RI, among other locations. About his artistic process, Barylick writes: "Each time a painting is begun, I want to go somewhere new, to surprise and shock myself. I'm an adventurer. I respond to what I find."

Mary Buchinger (Bodwell) is the author of both *Aerialist* (finalist for the May Swenson Poetry Award/ Utah State University Press; semi-finalist for the OSU Press/ *The Journal* Wheeler Prize and the Perugia Press Prize) and *Roomful of Sparrows* (Finishing Line Press). Her work has appeared in various anthologies and journals, including *AGNI, DIAGRAM, Homesickness and Exile* (Emma Press, England), *Nimrod, PANK, Salamander, The Anthology of New England Writers, The Cortland Review, The Massachusetts Review*. She was an invited reader at the Library of Congress and recipient of the Daniel Varoujan and Firman Houghton Awards from the New England Poetry Club, a Cambridge Poetry Award, and a prize from The Poetry Society of Virginia. She grew up on a family farm in the thumb area of Michigan and served as an agriculture volunteer in the Peace Corps in Ecuador. She holds a Ph.D. in applied linguistics from Boston University and is Associate Professor of English and Communication Studies at MCPHS University. She lives in Cambridge, Massachusetts, with her husband and two sons, two tuxedo cats, and a dog named Dover.

CPSIA information can be obtained at www.ICGtesting.com
Printed in the USA
BVOW05s1250110316

439882BV00002B/11/P